How to Be More Patient

An Essential Guide to Replacing Impatience with Patience

by **Greg Souchester**

Table of Contents

Introduction

They say that patience is a virtue, and while that sounds terribly pious and old fashioned, it turns out to be true.

In the late '60s, Stanford University did a study on pre-school children. They were given a marshmallow and were told that if they didn't eat it right away, they'd get more later. About half of the children couldn't wait, so they ate the marshmallow as soon as the teachers' backs were turned. The other half did wait and were rewarded with a second treat for their patience. Decades later, a follow-up showed that the children who waited to eat that marshmallow actually got better SAT scores, got better jobs with better salaries, and generally had better, more well-balanced, and more successful lives.

So is patience just about delaying immediate gratification? Simply put — yes. It's a lot more than just that, of course, but it makes for a good start.

In today's culture of instant gratification where credit cards allow you to pay with money you don't yet have, where articles have to be short or you'll never read them, where you spend more time deleting emails you won't read so you can get to those you need to, and where you can stay in touch with so-called "friends" you couldn't wait to forget about when you graduated: patience has become a dying art.

We've been trained to want something five minutes ago, though yesterday would be even better. Fortunately, there's Amazon and DSL, but even they can only go so far.

Impatience is becoming ingrained in us, and it's not working. There's a growing mountain of evidence from around the world which proves that effective multi-tasking simply does not exist. The more you try to do things simultaneously, the less effective and less productive you become, and the results tend to be inferior. Trying to make up for it by doing even more doesn't work — it only makes things worse and you get frazzled and stressed.

From a health perspective, impatience contributes to stress, high blood pressure, and premature aging, among other adverse effects. From a psychological standpoint, impatience leads to unnecessary risks and poor decisions. From a social point of view, being impatient is a guaranteed way of losing friends and making enemies. It's also just not very attractive.

And since you're no longer a pre-schooler, the stakes are now much higher than losing an extra marshmallow!

While circumstances and medication can affect your moods, you have far greater control over your own character than you probably care to admit. Fortunately for you, your attitude and knee jerk reactions are not set in stone. What you've learned can be unlearned. Even better, your bad habits can be replaced by good ones.

It takes patience, of course, but this book is here to help. Let's get started already!

Chapter 1: Defining Patience

Patience, at its best, is the ability to remain calm and tranquil while waiting for something to happen. It's the mental and emotional ability to accept that some things take time. Most importantly, it's the ability to understand that you are not the center of the universe, that things don't revolve around you, and that neither people nor the cosmos owes you anything. Certainly not right away.

Patience is the ability to accept that the people behind that McDonuts counter screwed up, but to err is human, so they don't deserve to get punched — emotionally satisfying though that would be. Good lawyers are so expensive these days and who wants to spend the night behind bars?

Unfortunately, patience at its best is something that only a few people are capable of, like Mahatma Gandhi and Mother Theresa. With enough practice (and patience), you can join their ranks later, but it's good to learn how to walk before you run.

Fortunately, there's a middle way to understand and practice patience. It's the ability to tolerate unpleasant conditions and to persevere when things aren't going too well or according to plan. More importantly, it's the ability to remain centered when life throws an unexpected wrench into the machinery of your carefully orchestrated schedule.

If you're stuck in traffic, for example, screaming your head off and honking your horn like crazy solves nothing. Intellectually, you know this. How you feel emotionally, is another matter. What you do about how you feel, is yet another.

Consider the following: you're stuck in traffic, but it doesn't bother you (maybe because you're listening to wonderful, inspiring music). All of a sudden, the car behind you starts honking and the guy behind the wheel keeps yelling, as if the traffic were your fault and as if you could do something about it. If that other driver did it long enough, how would you feel?

Intimidated? Harassed? Annoyed? Whatever the case, you'll eventually find your calm and good mood ruined, right? So there's another component to patience. It's the ability to understand that for better or worse, your emotions and the actions they inspire (if any) have an impact on others.

Understanding the five points below will help you become more patient:

(1) Things happen which are beyond your control,

(2) Whether or not you accept that fact, they will continue to happen

(3) Everything unpleasant has an end,

(4) Your feelings influence your actions, and you can learn to be better in-tune with your feelings.

(5) Your feelings and actions have a very real impact on yourself and others.

Chapter 2: Understanding What Patience Isn't

The reason patience sometimes gets associated with a certain four-letter word is because of how it's been misused. Wives have been told to be patient with their abusive husbands, victims have been told to be patient with the justice system, while the poor and oppressed have been told to be patient and pray. And now, we're being told to be patient with the banks and over tax cuts for high-income earners.

There's an old saying that goes *"All good things come to those who wait."* What a load of nonsense. Simply waiting, by itself, accomplishes nothing. Jobs come to those who look for them, money comes to those who work for it, opportunities come to those who make things happen, and results come to those who persist.

Some people think they're being patient by waiting for the right moment or for the right offer, etc. They're simply procrastinating, of course; possibly as a result of laziness or fear. To hide this fact, they tout patience as a virtue, abusing its true meaning.

Patience is not an excuse to opt out of something because it's difficult, inconvenient, or frightening. The activist and author

George Lester Jackson said that patience *"...has its limits. Take it too far, and it's cowardice."*

Patience is not about passivity, nor is it about being a doormat, a beggar with your hand out, or being lazy. Neither is it a quality for cloistered, religious orders out in the middle of nowhere.

Passivity is a conscious decision to do nothing, to avoid involvement, and is an attempt to hunker down and lie low. *ouch!* In many cases, it is indeed a form of cowardice or laziness. Patience, on the other hand, is the emotional decision to put up with something, however inconvenient. That decision to put up with something, however, is not meant to be forever.

The word "patience" carries with it an expectation of a result. You can tolerate standing in line patiently because you know you'll get to the end of it eventually. Doing so can be boring, can hurt your legs, and you no doubt have better things to do with your time. But the knowledge that you'll eventually get there is what sustains you.

Even in cases where waiting produces no results, the attempt to achieve one is often enough. Everyone who goes to a job interview, for example, knows that their chances of getting hired are 50/50. The important thing is that they put themselves out there, and in doing so, chose to be active rather than passive.

Patience is not about inactivity. It is the controlled expectation of a tangible result at best, or the hope of one at worst.

Chapter 3: Impatience and Its Benefits

Impatience isn't necessarily a bad thing. It isn't. Really! So long as you can keep a grip on it.

Impatience can be a motivating factor, as well as an agent for positive change. Although the Arab Spring in late 2010 took everyone outside the Middle East and North Africa by surprise, those who lived there were anything but.

While the desire to preserve traditional values and the rule of autocratic rulers kept most people in line, such factors could only hold them back for so long. The desire for social, political, and economic change had been brewing in the Arab world for decades. It was impatience that shook off their fear, bringing down dictators and forcing those still in power to bring about long overdue changes.

Impatience allows you to maintain focus on what you want. It also forces you to confront an unpleasant situation which, if unpleasant enough, requires you to act — hopefully in a positive way. The Civil Rights Movement is only one of many such examples.

Perhaps the most positive thing that can be said about impatience (if controlled) is how it can inspire creativity and improvement. In 2011, Denny Strigl, former president and CEO of Verizon Wireless, was asked how he managed to turn the company around. He said he hated waiting, inefficiency, and getting the runaround. His impatience with the Verizon people was not because he wanted to put them down, however, but rather because he knew they could do better. Once he was able to get that message across, his staff was inspired to improve — not just themselves, but the company as well.

Much of the new technology we have today was inspired by other people's impatience. There are apps that allow you to compare prices, get discounts, pick dates, etc. All of these are designed to save time, make things more convenient, and hopefully, lessen the inconveniences which make us impatient.

There is also the time element involved. Driving someone to the hospital because they're in a critical condition makes you want to drive faster, avoid distractions, and stay on track. In such a situation, impatience with traffic is perfectly justifiable and understandable.

It could even explain why the guy (or gal) behind you is honking his (or her) horn and yelling obscenities at you. If so, then that person is no longer in control of their impatience. Their impatience is controlling them. Then again, it's possible they're not actually yelling and honking at you, but at some cop ahead that you can't see.

This brings us to yet another important factor which can help you stretch your patience: *understanding where others are coming from.*

Chapter 4: Taking Control through Mindful Awareness

We are all born impatient; how we were raised determines whether or not impatience becomes our dominant quality. As infants, we wanted to be picked up, comforted, fed, or have our diapers changed right away.

As we grew older, things (hopefully) changed, but the speed and frequency with which our wants and needs were met had a cumulative effect. That aside, no one is either patient or impatient all the time. Even saints can lose their tempers and even the most impatient person has patient moments.

Experts say that your upbringing, your culture, and your environment have certainly contributed to your dominant personality today. But they also insist that your choices, conscious and otherwise, have also had an effect.

In Strigl's case, he claims to be in control of his impatience, citing it as a tool for self motivation, as well as one he uses to improve people and organizations. Assuming he's right and assuming that the people around him aren't miserable, then he clearly knows what he's doing and is therefore in control of his own character. If you can say the same for yourself, then you probably don't need to be reading this. Chances are, however, that your impatience has had a negative impact on your life, on your relationships, and on your finances.

There's an old Chinese saying that goes: *"One moment of patience may ward off great disaster. One moment of impatience may ruin a whole life."*

No doubt you can recall several incidents in your life where that saying holds true? Before you despair, look again. You should also recall that there were times when you were able to maintain an incredible degree of patience, even when others around you lost their cool.

It might therefore help to list the types of situations and people that stretch your patience. Is it traffic? Long lines? Slow workers? Telemarketers?

We all get impatient with such things and people, but attempt to pinpoint exactly what it is about these things that upset you so much? Often, your dominant personality makes you react to things automatically, even though you may not really understand why.

To get a grip on your dominant emotions and possibly change them, you first have to take a step back and get a good look at yourself. By writing down the things that trigger your impatience and to what degree they do so, you take the first step in understanding what affects you emotionally.

Dealing with What Causes Impatience

Assuming you've written out your list and your reasons, take another sheet of paper and divide it lengthwise into three columns. In the leftmost column, jot down the things you can control. In the rightmost column, write out the things you have no control over. Leave the middle blank for the moment.

Traffic is usually the number one item on most people's lists. The thought of sitting there doing nothing, feeling trapped since you can't move forward or back, but still having to pay for gas that isn't getting you anywhere is a guaranteed way to ruin anyone's day.

But let's say you've been taking that route regularly. If you know that rush hour starts at 6 every morning, for example, couldn't you try to wake up and leave a little earlier to avoid it? If this is something you can control, then put it on the left side. But if you live in Chicago, put it on the right side. Traffic in that city is virtually 24/7!

Now let's say you come across something you're not sure about. Put that in the middle. Go on with your list and feel free to keep switching stuff. If you don't fancy writing it out by hand, try using word processors like MS Word or Pages for Mac. You can also use Excel.

Once you've completed your list, take a look at those things you can (or think you can) control. Control means getting up earlier to avoid traffic (if possible), avoiding a certain route, person, or going to another Moonbucks outlet where the people aren't as slow and incompetent.

You might find that this requires massive changes on your part. If waking up earlier can solve the traffic problem for you, then you might have to go to bed sooner. Sometimes, a simple change, such as getting more sleep or avoiding caffeine past a certain hour, can do wonders for your patience meter.

Impatience usually arises because we feel we have no control over the situation. If you're dreading a meeting, for example, then getting stuck in traffic can be a welcome relief as it buys you time and delays the inevitable. But if you'll get dinged at work for being late again, but are still stuck in traffic, then that's another matter entirely.

By trying to identify the things you can control (albeit with some extra effort on your part), you begin to get a grip on the situation. This allows you to feel more empowered, reducing the causes of your impatience.

There's no way you can control everything, of course, and even the things you try to plan for can go awry. Fortunately, there are strategies for that, as well.

Chapter 5: Quick and Easy Ways to Exercise Patience

The causes of stress, anxiety, and impatience are the same. They come about because of your fight or flight response. This was how our ancestors survived wild beasts before we came up with the brilliant idea of putting them into zoos or rendering them extinct.

When confronted by danger, our ancestors were faced with two options: stay and fight the problem (and possibly have a meal) or run like hell. Today, our problems are a little more complex, but the mechanism remains the same. The following options are today's more evolved responses to stress that will help you become more patient:

Take a Deep Breath

They say that breath is life, but did you know that it's also an excellent stress buster?

When stressed, anxious, or impatient, we start to breathe quickly and more shallowly. This sends adrenalin flowing through our bodies, giving us more energy so we can either do battle or run away from one.

This can be hard to do in a car and embarrassing (or illegal) in a line, but cars and lines are relatively new things, you understand? This is why some people actually like being impatient or annoyed — they feel it empowers them. They thrive off the energy boost they get when yelling at (or attacking) McDonuts employees who work too slowly or get orders wrong.

Adrenalin, however, is like an energy drink in that what goes up must come down. This is why energy drinks are a bad idea. When your body burns through the sugar in an energy drink, it starts to crash (never mind the exact medical terminology). Similarly, when that adrenalin rush passes, your body enters a low, rendering you tired, sleepy, and feeling dull.

So the next time you find yourself gritting your teeth because of impatience, take a deep, long breath. Then take another one, and yet another. In fact, try it now. Feels wonderful, doesn't it?

No, you are not being impressionable. It really works because you can't take a single deep breath and several shallow ones at the same time. Shallow breaths trigger excitement, whereas a single deep one does the opposite. That deep breath triggers your vagus nerve which in turn slows down your heart rate. This tells your brain that the "danger" has passed, so you feel a sense of relief that it's over.

The next time you find yourself getting impatient over something, relax, take a deep breath, and repeat as often as necessary. It doesn't matter if that car keeps honking, if that guy keeps yelling, and if that line still isn't moving. Just keep breathing slowly and deeply — it is you, not anything or anyone else, that matters.

Tell a Different Story

In that Stanford "marshmallow test", the children who waited patiently for more treats survived the waiting period by playing mind games with themselves. Some cuddled their marshmallows as if they were pets, others viewed it strategically because they wanted more, and so on. Whatever they did, they were clearly intelligent enough to realize that a little patience now would lead to greater rewards later. It probably explains why the impatient children likely ended up behind the McDonuts counter.

Impatience begins as a form of mental anguish that begins to infect your body, making it tense and uncomfortable. Since we don't like discomfort, we want it to end. When it doesn't, we want to blame something or someone for our distress. Lashing out provides some form of emotional relief, even if it results in embarrassing or terrible consequences later.

If you pay attention to your next episode of impatience, you might realize that it all begins with a sort of barely verbalized dialogue that goes on in your head. If you're waiting in a very slow moving line, for example, you'll notice that after a few minutes of genuine patience, you start breathing a little faster and your body starts getting tense.

Looking over to the front of the line, the people there start annoying you, even if you've never met them before or never will. A dialogue starts forming in your head, something along the lines of "*come on, hurry up!*" If you let this go on, it gets even more dramatic, emotional, and vicious. This in turn makes you tense up even more, creating a mind-body loop of increasing tension, stress, and annoyance.

The solution is to tell yourself a different story. Rather than carry on with the dialogue about how the universe is out to get you by putting you in the slowest line, remind yourself how lucky you are to have a bank balance (assuming you're in a bank) or that you can afford to buy food (if you're at a store or fast food joint).

Try to spend your waiting time being grateful for the opportunity to rethink that business plan or proposal, or that speech you've been working on to justify a raise. Having something interesting to read on you can also make a wait seem much shorter. By maximizing your mind's potential and keeping it busy with something productive, you bypass your natural tendency for negative dialogue. In so doing, you also bypass your tendency toward impatience over something you have no control over.

Getting a grip on your own internal dialogue can be difficult in the beginning, but practice really does make perfect. The trick is to engage your thoughts in something that really interests you so that you don't let yourself slide back into impatience.

Whenever your mind and body starts getting riled up again, take a few deep breaths and get back to that interesting story.

Put Yourself in Another Person's Shoes

At the end of chapter 3, a scenario was given in which that annoying driver behind you wasn't referring to you at all but desperately trying to signal some cop you couldn't see. It's easy to believe you're the center of the universe and that things revolve around you. Consequently, it's only logical to believe that when things go wrong, it's the universe itself that's out to get you.

In that scenario, you're not actually a part of the picture. Shocking though this may sound, here's a newsflash for you: 99.99% of the time, you're not.

Imagine if the person behind you was trying to drive someone in a critical condition to the hospital. Also imagine that instead of honking at you, they were actually trying to get help from someone ahead of you... like an ambulance also stuck in traffic. If you knew that, would you still get annoyed and impatient with that driver?

That's only a scenario, of course. Most of the time, we can't know about other people's situations, what's going on in their heads, or even understand the overall picture. But just as you have your own life, it might help to know that others also have theirs.

The next time you start feeling impatient because of other people and telling yourself a different story doesn't work, try this — make up a story about the person or persons who are causing your annoyance.

If the person ahead of you has way too much in their shopping cart, imagine it's because they have a lot of mouths to feed and how difficult it must be for them. Whether it's true or not is not the point. The point is that although you can't possibly know a stranger's story, you acknowledge that they have one, just like you do.

It's easy to get impatient with perfect strangers because to you, they're usually just moving obstacles in your way. To them, that's all you probably are, as well.

If that person ahead of you was someone you cared about, wouldn't you feel less annoyed (if at all) about the fact that they're slowing the line down? Of course you would.

By trying to tell their story (even though you're only making it up), you humanize them. In so doing, you realize they're not deliberately trying to ruin your day. Like you, they're simply trying to get by.

Making up a sympathetic story about others allows you to put yourself in their shoes. In doing so, you take the first steps in giving them the same patience and understanding that you would want others to show you.

Be Present

Often, we worry about things that haven't happened yet. If something were already happening, we wouldn't be worrying — we'd probably be suffering.

The next time you find yourself getting impatient over something, take a deep breath and take a closer look at the situation. Let's go back to the stuck-in-traffic example. So there you are getting annoyed because you're trapped. Besides the obvious, what's upsetting you? Is it because your legs hurt? Is it because you're about to be late for work? Is it because you feel being trapped pretty much sums up your life?

Except for the fact that your legs hurt, the other two have no immediate impact on your present. Think about it. It could be that being late could cost you your job, but it hasn't happened yet, now has it? It could indeed be true that being trapped sums up your life. But if so, then even if the traffic suddenly vanished, your life would still be the same, wouldn't it?

Your impatience, annoyance, and worry are not usually about what's happening in the present. They're usually about your fear of the future. If you can get your mind to focus on the present, you can deal with the discomforts of the present. If your legs hurt because you've been riding the clutch for too long (assuming you're driving a manual), then brake, sit back, and start massaging your legs.

Take a look around you. See if you can spot a driver who attracts you, a child's face you find adorable, a cool car, a funny bumper sign, etc. Every moment of every single day is filled with delight, if you but take the time to notice. You can only notice, however, if you drag your mind away from the past or back from the future and bring it firmly into the now.

Being present also means letting go. Say you will get fired because the traffic will make you late... again. The heck can you do about it there and then? If you can call your boss and if s/he will accept your excuse, then fine. If not, then seriously, what else can you do? Worrying about finding a new job, how you'll make the next car payment, and so on, is letting your mind wander off toward the future once more. Stop and get back to the present.

The only thing you can do is be in the present moment. With the exception of aching legs, accept the now and do what you can to appreciate the things around you. Understanding and accepting that you can only do so much can be a very liberating feeling. It is not about letting go of responsibility. It is about knowing that you've done what you could and the rest is beyond your control.

Chapter 6: Being Patient with Yourself

The previous chapters all focused on being patient with situations and with other people. So now let's focus on you. Whether its self-improvement, vying for a promotion, learning a new language or skill — you want to get somewhere, or get something, or be someone, but it's not happening fast enough for you.

So you feel impatient with yourself.

First off, that's a good thing. That impatience drives you, keeps you focused on your goal, and (hopefully) forces you to be creative and come up with new strategies to get what you want. So long as that impatience keeps you on track, it'll remain a good thing.

When that impatience turns to despair and anger however, aah... then that's something else entirely. That's another internal dialogue right there that you've allowed to get out of control.

So first, remember to take a deep breath. Next, make a progress chart by getting out another sheet of paper and dividing it lengthwise into three columns. Title the leftmost column as "SHORT-TERM GOALS." The middle column's title should be "MIDTERM GOALS," and the rightmost column should be "LONG-TERM GOALS."

Say you're aiming for a promotion. Beneath the first column, write out the things you want to achieve that'll get you noticed. In the middle, list the positions immediately above you. In the third, write out the position you ultimately want (like CEO).

If possible, write out target dates next to each listing. These shouldn't be set in stone, but they can be used as a motivating factor. Constantly look at this list and update or make modifications as necessary.

By breaking down your goals into short-term, midterm, and long-term posts, you set yourself targets which hopefully inspire you. If things go awry or are delayed, approach it like a game. If you didn't get that promotion when you wanted it, for example, then come up with new strategies or new goals. Approaching it this way allows you to step back and approach the situation as logically as possible. When things don't go as planned, back off, breathe, reassess, and make whatever changes you see fit.

You can do this with virtually anything. This gives you a plan, a guide to your own life, if you will. By trying to take some measure of control over it and giving yourself measurable goals, you eliminate the randomness that sometimes causes despair.

Conclusion

Impatience isn't always a bad thing, so long as you can keep it under control. Chronic impatience, on the other hand, is damaging to your physical, emotional, and mental health. It also often results in losses and in delays — which is exactly what you are impatiently trying to avoid in your hurry.

Your mental habits, which you've built up over many years, are at the root of impatience. Fortunately, just as habits can be formed, so they can be unformed, if you but try. To do so, you must first become aware of what's going on in your head and try to identify those things which really work you up.

It helps to know you're not the center of the universe, that you can't control everything, and that other people have as much right to happiness as you do. Be patient with yourself and resolve to forgive yourself for your past impatient outbursts as you begin to create a new you following the tips in this book.

Developing patience doesn't happen overnight, of course. It takes time and a tremendous amount of effort. When you do learn to stretch your patience, the rewards and joy of knowing you are in control of your emotions will be more than worth it.

Finally, I'd like to thank you for purchasing this book! If you enjoyed it or found it helpful, I'd greatly appreciate it if you'd take a moment to leave a review on Amazon. Thank you!

Made in the USA
Middletown, DE
05 April 2021